MY
MEMOIR
WORKBOOK

MY MEMOIR WORKBOOK
Created By
Marcia Rosen

abbott press®
A DIVISION OF WRITER'S DIGEST

My Memoir Workbook

Registered: Writer's Guild of America, East

Abbott Press books may be ordered through booksellers or by contacting:

Abbott Press
1663 Liberty Drive
Bloomington, IN 47403
www.abbottpress.com
Phone: 1-866-697-5310

ISBN: 978-1-4582-0301-4 (sc)
ISBN: 978-1-4582-0300-7 (e)

Printed in the United States of America

Abbott Press rev. date:5/11/2012

What is a Memoir?

It is a LifeStory

What is your *LifeStory*?

It is a story you write about your life and how you lived it

This workbook is dedicated to you!

Each of us has a history and our own unique story. From time to time, photographic slides of the past, of both good and bad times, show in our mind. Memories continually dance around in our heads. There may come a time when you may want to preserve these unforgettable moments on paper. This Memoir Workbook was developed to help you capture those moments. Work at your own pace and in your own words.

Writing a memoir can be a daunting and, at times, emotional experience. It is also exciting, fulfilling and rewarding. A memoir is a true story you tell about specific events, experiences or times in your life. You can write about the whole span of your life or one specific episode.

Perhaps you want to write a book that might help or inspire others outside your circle of family and friends. You may want to write down your experiences to heal your own soul or come to terms with a difficult emotional past. You may simply want to leave a lasting record that celebrates your life!

This workbook will help you create a record and a legacy of your life for your family. Children, grandchildren and other relatives will enjoy learning about your life. Provide generations to come a history of what you contributed to your family and your community. Tell them how you lived your life and the truths about your choices and experiences. Show them how you faced life's joys and challenges. Share how you loved, cried, struggled and survived it all.

Whatever the reason, in this workbook you will tell your story, your version of your life as it was experienced by you. This is your book, to tell about your life in your own voice, to relay your message and share your vision. This workbook will provide you with the inspiration, motivation and encouragement to finish the task. Don't keep your memories hidden inside any longer.

This workbook also provides tips for remembering pieces of your story; how to use your own voice; how to maintain a flow to keep the information connected and meaningful; and how to move past limiting mindsets, attitudes and emotions so you do not get paralyzed...so you write your truth from your heart and soul.

So, turn the page and start the great and exciting adventure of writing your LifeStory!

*Buy a beautiful notebook or journal and start writing
*Make a list of important dates and events in your life
*Make a list of your life experiences
*Jog your memory with photos and mementos
*Gather pertinent information
*Research as many details as you possibly can
*Search old newspaper stories
*Recall historical events
*Research on familytree.com
*Determine your goals in writing your LifeStory
*Write what inspires you
*Decide if you want to write about one particular time, or event, or about your entire life
*Prepare to tell the truth
*Think of your life in terms of all five senses: touch, taste, sound, smell and sight
*Read several memoirs and identify what it is you like about them
*Don't let the negative opinions of others deter you
*Write everyday
*Enter writing contests
*Write articles
*Seek professional assistance developing your memoir
*Seek professional assistance with writing, editing, proofreading, publishing and marketing your book
*Keep writing!

****

What to do Next?
*Explore marketing opportunities
*Utilize the internet and social media to promote yourself and your book
*Create a buzz about your work if you want to sell your book
*Learn what is new in book publishing and e-books

Table of Contents

YOUR MEMOIR WORKBOOK

Working Title_____

By_____

1. Information Gathering Process

Getting started is often the hardest thing to do. Now is the time to take that first step, write that first sentence, and know you are about to visit a past that has brought you to this time and this place. Some of it will be emotional and challenging and some of it will be joyful!

Why do you want to write a book? What is your motivation?

What concerns, fears, and issues do you have about writing your memoir?

What kind of memoir do you want to write? Will you write about the whole of your life or a specific episode?

Do you want to write the book on your own or work with a ghostwriter?

Who is your audience?

2. Where to Start

Look through your journals, notebooks and diaries. Look through old and newer photo albums, scrapbooks and places where you have kept mementos of your life. Use these things to remind you of images, dates, people and places that you may want to include in your book. It is important to collect these memories before beginning the process of writing your LifeStory.

If you have concerns and are feeling unsure about writing your LifeStory please know that we all have negative voices in our head. This is the time for you to tell these voices they are no longer welcome. Maybe they've been critical and holding you back for far too long. Simply tell them to go away! This is your time, and you want to make the most of it.

Exercise:
Where will you collect your ideas? Who can you talk to that might share some memories with you? Make a list of items you can review, people you can talk to and places where you can find more about your memories.

Now, write a letter of 50 words or less to anyone you want, which describes some part of your LifeStory. (Write in your notebook or journal more letters of any length to other people, this is a great way to find your voice and explore expressing yourself openly and honestly).

3. The Process

Develop some basic concepts for your book. Determine if it will be serious, humorous, or sad. Will you structure it as a series of short stories within one book? Will it be chronological, beginning at a certain age, and looking back at the span of your life?

How do you envision your book format and structure? Will you divide your story into chapters or sections?

.

.

.

What point of view, tone and voice do you want to present? Will your story be happy, angry, reflective, wishful, grieving, or sad? Find your truth and trust your voice. It's your story!

.

.

.

Aside from yourself, who are the primary characters in your LifeStory?

.

.

.

List a few possible ideas for the title of your memoir.

.

.

.

4. Beginnings

Thoughts on Why You Are Writing Your LifeStory

To Remember You...To Think About You...To Give Voice to Your Life

To Leave a Legacy for Your Loved Ones, Friends and Others

To Inspire, Motivate and Encourage

To Grieve...To Heal...To Release Yourself From Hurts, Pains and Sorrows

To Tell Your Truths...To Make Others Accountable to Their Truths

To Search for Answers...To Understand Them

To Find Comfort

To Find Joy and Celebration in All You Are and All You Have Done

To Honor Your Accomplishments

Exercise:
On the next page write a first line for your LifeStory, then 50-100 words using one of the following prompts:

*I remember.
*Once upon a time.
 *Happiness/Sadness to me is
*Love/Hate to me is.
*I miss.
*We ended it and I felt...
*The stress was...
*The hurt was...
*The grief was...
*The cold, the heat, the wind, the rain, the view, the smell, remind me of...
*It was very confusing that day, that time, that experience
*Why did that person behave like that? Say that?
*I see it all clearly now and...
        ...Or, Write about something that made you feel sad, mad or happy

Ideas for my first sentence...you can start by using several of the prompts suggested on the previous page.

Write your first 50-100 words here.

Ask yourself why you chose a certain prompt? What about it describes your story? Does it take you through the first steps of what you want your memoir to be about?

5. Point-of-View, Tone
and Character Development

Point of View is the description of what is going on in the main character's head. Since you are writing a memoir, the point of view and the tone in which you present it should reflect your thoughts and feelings about a given situation...fear, anger, happiness, confusion, surprise, tenderness, comfort, joy, etc. Make an effort to stay in your own point of view at all times as this makes your images more vivid.

Character development should include how a person looks - their physical appearance in general including the color of their hair and eyes, their height, their age. Information about their attitude, the place they live, their work or profession should be included. Equally important is your impression of the motivation of the other characters in your life, and their relationship to your story.

Exercise:

Create a character development sketch and summarize the point of view for at 3 of the characters in your book. Your reader should be able to visualize each character. On the next page use the following question to write about your characters:

*What is the <u>most</u> important thing to know about each character?

*How do they look? What do they like to wear? What are their ages?

* What are the colors of their hair and eyes, and their overall physical traits?

*Are they married, single, divorced, or widowed?

*Do they have children, and if so, what are their ages?

*How do they feel about life, love, marriage, children, etc.?

*What are their good and bad character traits?

*What are their occupations, hobbies, interests, etc.?

*What are their relationships and reactions to each other...and to you?

*How has this character impacted your LifeStory?

Character 1:

Character 2:

Character 3:

6. Creating Your Structure

Now that you have some ideas about the basic format, structure, flow, tone, voice, point of view and characters that you want in your book...it is time to get serious about writing! Using your ideas for a first sentence, and the writing prompt for your first paragraph, begin writing your story and your book.

Exercise:

Write the "first" pages of your prologue, introduction or first chapter, using the first paragraph from Chapter 4. Start here, continue on to the next blank writing pages.

7. Backstory

Backstory is what happened before your story begins. It includes your characters' backgrounds, the stories that they carry around in their heads and the events that shaped them. The backstory should be included in small doses and only when necessary. The inclusion of the backstory usually works best if inserted in the first half of the book closer to the middle, rather than in the very beginning or end. However, don't allow the backstory to drag down the pace of your main story.

Writing any backstory requires a delicate balance. Too much, and the story bogs down. Not enough, and your reader won't understand your characters' motivation. You might want to "hold on" to a dramatic piece of the backstory for the end, this is called a reveal and is an excellent way to create a cliffhanger! Some methods of inserting the backstory are through flashbacks, discussions between characters, or a very short summary of a past action that had a significant impact.

Exercise:

Identify some characters in your backstory, their character traits and history, and their actions. Make them interesting and tell how they relate to your story. Begin here and continue on the next blank writing page.

8. Summary or Outline of Your LifeStory

Now that you have developed some of your characters, your point of view and tone, your backstory and written your first page, you are ready to create the <u>heart</u> of your LifeStory. Use this space to write a summary or outline of your LifeStory. Don't worry about grammar or spelling...write without editing. All that can be done later. This should be the roadmap to your story, but know that you can always change direction.

Include the essential elements of your memoir:

*The structure from the beginning to the end of the book.

*A prologue, should you decide to use one can, create a sense of interest and anticipation about your story.

*If you want to include an introduction it should explain a little about the book and why you are writing it.

*Decide whether you will divide your manuscript into chapters or sections. How will you structure each chapter? Will it be divided into years, life experiences, events or time periods?

* Who are the primary characters and the backstory characters?

*What will your conclusion consist of? Where you are now, what do you feel is most important to you?

Several blank writing pages follow so you can develop your summary or outline. You may want to write in pencil. Remember that rewrites are a part of writing any book. Please note, there is NO right way to write your story. You have a lifetime of experiences to share.

My Memoir Story
Summary/Outline

9. Memoir Checklist

Make the Memories of Your Life...Memorable!

- Remember: Write often! If possible, set aside a time to write daily.
- Is your "first" sentence interesting, compelling, inviting to the reader?
- Are you happy with the tone, point of view, characters and structure of your story?
- Have you used your voice? Remember, it's your story.
- Is there interesting and insightful dialogue?
- Does the story flow with continuity of your intent throughout?
- Have you carefully researched the facts and been truthful?
- Did you add some of the backstory of your life?
- Have you made the memories of your life memorable for the reader?
- If possible, have someone read your memoir aloud to you.
- It may take several drafts before your LifeStory is ready for the next steps.
- In revised drafts, ask yourself what should be added and deleted.
- Find professional help in editing, and proofreading.
- Proofread carefully for grammar, punctuation and spelling errors.
- Have a professional guide you through the publishing process.
- Write about any part of your LifeStory that moves your heart and soul and that allows you to give voice to the stories you have longed to tell!

10. Keeping Motivated, Inspired and Encouraged

If you are feeling paralyzed or experiencing anxiety about writing, it may be time to slow down or take a step back. Or, maybe it's time to work with some of the writing prompts on this page to help you get the words flowing again. Many writers experience writer's block at times.

Writing exercises and prompts can also help you to enhance your writing skills and allow you to escape for a time from thinking about your memoir. These exercises allow you to view situations and people from different perspectives and even to expand your memoir. These exercises and prompts will give you new ideas, so have some fun with them. Respond to any or all of them and don't be concerned about how what you write fits into your book.

More Writing Exercises and Prompts

• Pick three people you know and write a brief paragraph about each of them.

• Select five of your favorite words and write a paragraph with each word in it.

• What is your favorite TV show? Write an idea for it.

• Write about someone who was in your life when you were a teenager.

• When you are in your favorite coffee shop or café, look around you, and write about the people and what they are doing.

• Write a letter to your favorite author and tell them how much you admire their work.

• Write a letter to anyone you wish you had shared your feelings with.

• Write about something you might be grieving about. Any loss deserves to be grieved.

• Write about how you see the world today.

• Write something funny and keep at it for 15 minutes.

• Write 10 words only about how you feel about the memoir you are writing.

Your Writing Prompt Pages

11. Writing Your Memoir – How to Follow Through to Completion

You know who you are, your goals, and your storyline, now it's time to complete your memoir!

- Take everything you've written in the memoir workbook and organize your manuscript.
- It may help to have a notebook with dividers to separate the prologue, introduction, chapters, etc.
- You can also set up files and folders on your computer.
- By dividing the memoir into sections you can fill in the pieces of your story as you write them.
- As you transfer information from your *My Memoir Workbook* you can add or delete content and do some minor editing.
- The process of organizing your manuscript allows you the opportunity to once again review your concept and storyline.
- Take your time.
- Have a professional edit your work.
- Write from your heart, from your voice, from your LifeStory!

12. Some Reminders...and a Few More Things You Should Know

A little bit of wisdom and sound advice to help you create a wonderful, well-written, skillfully edited memoir.

Opening Lines that Work

Like first impressions, first lines DO matter. They draw in your reader and set the tone for your first paragraph and your entire book. You want to set off in the right direction, capture your reader and have your voice, point of view and a compelling hint of the tone of the book show through. Be willing to revisit your opening lines as your book progresses.

More About Your Characters

What do your characters want? What makes them behave and say what they do? Your readers should have an emotional response to your characters, either good or bad. Your characters should be motivated by something they want, care about and are searching for longing for. Remember to describe the characters including their appearance, age, behavior and educational background. Are your characters religious or bohemian types? You get the idea! Know your characters' voices. Do you want readers to like them, feel sorry for them or love them? Are they interesting, humorous, serious, sarcastic, difficult, kind, etc.? Do not forget while you are doing this to include yourself; after all, *you are* the primary character!

Dialogue

We communicate all the time. Our words are usually our connection to others and they can make a significant and long lasting impact. Be careful and thoughtful in your narrative. Make it smooth and interesting and make it sound real as relates to your characters. Create an interesting exchange between your characters.

Point of View...Do's and Don'ts

Do try to be consistent.

Don't switch back and forth from first person to third person.

Don't try to please everyone.
It's your book, your story, go with what feels right.

How "NOT" to Write a Memoir

Don't wait to be inspired. Your inspiration is already inside you.
Do not try to copy/line edit as you go along.
Do not try to fit into trends that may not fit your style or interests.
Over-planning, over-researching, or relying on other's opinion of your work, can cause your work to feel artificial.

Concept Editing

This is an important element in the development of your book and is designed to help you be sure you are maintaining a consistency in the structure, tone and flow of your book. Copy and line editing should be done when you have completed your manuscript.

Copy and Line Editing

Copy and line editing reviews for style, including grammar, punctuation, spelling and -transitions. You want your manuscript to be perfect before it goes to a publisher or agent.

Proofreading

Proofreading is the final phase; your work should be polished and ready for a final read through. You decide who to ask to proofread; it can be a friend, a writing instructor/consultant, a professional editor or anyone you trust to be careful and thorough.

Print Proof

Once your book has come back from the publisher with the proper cover design and text format, it is necessary to once again line edit and proofread your book to be sure the publisher or printer has not made any errors, deleted words or paragraphs and that spacing, fonts, headings and general structure are consistent.

13. Organizing Your Book for Publication

Once you've completed writing and a first edit of your book, there is more work to do. It's all part of the process of publishing a book. It is very helpful to do a mock-up including each of the following sections (1-11). You may find yourself doing several mock-ups until you are satisfied with the basic format you want. Select several of your favorite books and examine their format and style. Ask yourself what you like about the size, paper color and texture, the cover and inside design concept? You might choose ideas from several books. The exercise below will help you make some of those decisions.

1. Cover: Title and Author

2. Inside Front Page: About the Book

3. Publisher Page(s): ISBN, Bar Code and Copyright, etc.

4. Acknowledgments

5. Prologue

6. Introduction

7. Sections and/or Chapters (With cover page and heading for each section or chapter)

8. Epilogue (If desired)

9. Inside Back Page: About the Author With Photo

10. Back Cover: Title, Testimonial Blurbs

11. Set the price of your book with the help of your publisher and marketing advisor.

Exercise:
Create the mock-up of your book as suggested above.
Take blank sheets of paper and fold in half, giving you 4 sides.
Now create mock-up and layout with estimated number of pages for your book.
You may do this a number of times until you are satisfied.
This will also help you know how much more you might want to write.

14. Publishing and Marketing Your Memoir

While many of you are using this workbook to help you develop and write your memoir for family, friends and loved ones, some of you may want to explore how to publish and promote your book to a broader audience. There are many opportunities for you to do this and following are some essentials for your success.

*Contact literary agents or publishers. There is a complete list in the annual "Literary Market Place" and "Writer's Market," which can be found at your local library. Check out agents or publishers that work with memoirs and remember to investigate Independent publishers and University Presses.

*Self-publishing has become an accepted way to publish your book or eBook. Are you willing to self-publish? Using a "Print on Demand" option, buy as few copies as possible at first. Carefully and thoroughly compare publishing options and costs. Ask for referrals for the most reliable and cost effective self-publishing companies.

*Register your work with the Writer's Guild of America, East or West. This is a very inexpensive and useful way to protect your work. Also, every book should have an ISBN registration. You can obtain an ISBN registration online or through your publisher.

*Self-published books can be promoted through many online sites (several of which are listed this workbook). Your book can also be marketed online through "Amazon Advantage", "Barnes and Noble Booksellers" and other places that you can find through Google. Social media such as Facebook and Twitter can also be a huge outlet for your book promotion. You need someone who knows how to utilize these powerful tools for marketing.

*How much effort and money are you willing to expend to help promote your book? How will you accomplish this? Would you be willing to participate in book signings, speaking engagements, use social media, create a website or hire a public relations consultant?

Exercise

Write an updated biography highlighting areas of your life that you would like to see on the author page of your book. Think about how this biography could help to promote sales of your memoir.

Resources

Read all kinds of memoirs. Learn from books about writing. Follow and read publications, websites and blogs that allow you to explore the world of writing and publishing.

Some Suggested Memoirs
Glass Castle by Jeanette Walls
A Mountain of Crumbs by Ellen Gorokhova
Let's Take the Long Way Home by Gail Caldwell
Making Toast by Roger Rosenblatt
Angela's Ashes by Frank McCourt
You're Old, I'm Old...Get Used to it by Virginia Ironside

Good Books on the Craft of Writing:
Unless It Moves The Human Heart by Roger Rosenblatt
On Writing: A Memoir of the Craft by Steven King
Bird by Bird by Anne Lamott
Old Friend From Far Away by Natalie Goldberg
Escaping into the Open by Elizabeth Berg
Women and Writing by Virginia Woolf

Helpful Publications:
Writer's Digest: www.writersdigest.com
WritersMarket: www.writersmarket.com
The Writer Magazine: www.writermag.com
Poets & Writers: www.pw.org
Book Business: www.bookbusinessmag.com

Useful Websites and Blogs
www.shewrites.com
www.goodreads.com
www.bookmovement.com
www.pagesfob.blogspot.com
www.fundsforwriters.com

A Story About Writing

I have been passionate about writing since I was a teenager and it has been a lifetime of loving words and the stories that come from putting words together. I love how words can change a life, can make someone feel wonderful or terrible, or, happy or sad. I loved, and still do, how words make sentences, then paragraphs, then stories and books and movies and so much more. And I love how words express stories, like yours, that tell of inner dreams and demons, of tragedies and truths, of heartbreak and hope.

My hope for now, is that this story I've written about writing helps you feel inspired to keep writing, to appreciate the process and to complete your memoir. I promise you it will make your heart sing to finish your book!

A COLLECTION OF PENS©
By
Marcia Rosen

I read a book that says writers can—and even should—write just about anywhere and everywhere. We should write in cafes, restaurants, and coffee shops; on buses, boats, trains, and planes; and where beauty surrounds us in museums, art galleries and places of worship.

Our minds can travel along with our physical beings so that our thoughts can become words that express ideas, which can be organized to form a book, article, play or script. When our words are grouped in such a work, they allow us to say, "I'm a writer."

What a lovely idea to be able to write anywhere! One can even compose comfortably in a public place in full view and with full view of passersby. We can watch people moving at their own pace giving us impressions and insights for stories and for characters whose voices and personas we want to create. Watching these passersby, we might ask ourselves: "Who are they? Where are they going? What are they thinking about? Are they wondering why I am watching them?"

We can write from the coffee shop down the street or from a café somewhere across the world. Sometimes we just move from idea to idea. Sometimes, in a precious moment, we find a concept that takes hold of us and we cannot let go of it until we have explored it and given it breath of life. Then we must determine whether we should support its development or let it die so we can move on unhampered to the next moment.

When I began to think about this, and then to write about such thoughts, I wondered, "Does it really matter where I write? There might be something special about a person or place that could become the focus of where I might begin, or even end, a story. However, the most important thing was not where I write, but that no matter where, I keep writing.

"I'm a writer," I repeat aloud to myself when no one is near to wonder whether I might be crazy. I introduce myself as a writer to people I've never before met. I need them to believe this. I need to have others believe it so I will also be convinced of its truth. Call it what you may: ego, desire, or wishful thinking.

Writing has been my heart's desire since I was a youth. "Such things are not important," I'd been told. I was raised in a home where there were no books, no music, and no one willing to help me believe in my dream. Remembering that now, as well as many times over the years, still makes my soul sad.

On a visit to a friend not so long ago, I thought about all this while sitting in a lovely guest room in an Inn in Vermont. It was a warm winter weekend, but spring had not yet touched the trees or grass. In Vermont, spring was still miles away. My friend would not be coming to meet me for a few hours, so I decided to write.

However, I realized I needed a pen. For some reason, I could not find any of the several pens I had brought with me. So, I went into the office like a pilot on a mission and helped myself to one of their free pens. With it already in my hand, I said to the desk clerk, "I'm taking one of your pens. Writers shouldn't be without a pen." She smiled in apathetic agreement.

I had noticed the pens when I walked into the lobby earlier that morning. There they were: Vermont green pens with white stenciling on them that promoted the Inn's name and phone number. Its web address was clearly imprinted on it as well. It's a new world.

Yes, I could have used my laptop. But it's just not the same. It's not the same to someone who feels about pen and paper the way I do. I write on lined pads of beautifully colored paper. I have them in purple and blue and pink. I love the way it feels when my pen touches the paper. I know that when the words appear they are from my voice. Sometimes the words and phrases seem to spread across the colored paper as if by magic!

It is right then and there in the Vermont Inn that I decide to begin "A Collection of Pens." It would be both a story and a real collection. I would collect pens from everywhere and anywhere that I wrote. Then, I would *write* about my collection of pens. "After all, I'm a *writer*."

I decided I would also buy a "special pen" in each city I visited. My collection of pens would remind me of the dream of my youth and the belief of that dream becoming reality in my older age. The pens would have been my paint brush if I had been an artist. They would have been my ballet slippers if I had been a ballerina.

My collection of pens is not meant to be displayed. I don't really need anyone else to see them. I certainly don't want anyone to touch them! In fact, there are only a few people to whom I might consider showing my treasures because for me they are precious. They allow my heart and soul to share my secrets and my truths. I hold them tightly when I'm writing for fear that if loosen my grip the ideas might escape. Then, how would I write?

When I hold a pen, it becomes my friend, my lover, my conscience. Sometimes I hold the pen in long embrace thinking about what I want to do next. Where do I want to go with my ideas or the relationship of my characters? The pen feels my emotions as I squeeze it, tap it, swirl it around, or even put it in my mouth. The pen knows my touch. We are intimate. The pen even knows when to be ruthless and unforgiving, grabbing hold of thoughts before they wander or lose their way.

Together, we are in this pursuit of words and sentences and paragraphs and pages and chapters that become a book filled with human dignities, and at times, even indignities. In books, we can find ourselves or lose ourselves. We might travel long distances or take short walks across time and place. We find expressions of all emotions and complications, as in many relationships. We wonder how it feels to be that person, in that place, in that time. We pretend and envision that we could lead that life and occupy a special place in the book.

My collection of pens has helped me open minds and hearts: Sometimes those of others, sometimes my own. I have thought quite seriously about what this collection of pens means to me. I understand clearly and certainly that it is about my promise to myself as a youth that, "I will one day be an important writer." I had envisioned my books in the windows of bookstores. I had seen myself signing books as a long line of waiting and eager readers came to the table with their purchase of my book and gave me their name to sign in their copy of it.

Today, when people at my book signings tell me about themselves and their dreams, I feel a connection. I understand their hunger. It was my hunger as well to have a dream fulfilled. Some ask me how long it takes to write a book. Others simply said: "Thank you, you're a wonderful writer." I beam. I reach out and touch their hand, look at them and say thank you. I really mean it. At the same time, I whisper to myself, "Dear God, thank you for this gift."

My collection of pens has helped me to reach the dream that appeared to me so long ago. They have been my support and my determination. Too often we writers do not have people who encourage us. Sometimes we have one or two, but it is not always enough. People in our lives tell us we are foolish or unrealistic. We often give them too much power.

To this day, that awful voice with the destructive words and attitude has never quite left me. People who should have supported me said: "Who do you think you are?" Although I long ago beat it, drowned it and buried it beneath layers of hopefulness, now and then, that voice creeps to the surface. I answer by reminding myself of my accomplishments: "I'm a writer. I not only have my collection of pens, I also have the books and stories I've written to prove it."

Keep Writing....
Reminders•Notes•Random Thoughts for My Memoir

Encouraging and Supporting the Writer Within You!

Literary Agent for Self-Published Authors
Published Author, Book Advisor and Consultant
For
Writers of memoirs, fiction and non-fiction books

Available for Workshop Programs and Speaking Presentations
Founder, Creative Book Concepts

In writing my memoir "Life Savors", Marcia was invaluable in helping me. Marcia, your clarity of vision in terms of a "through-line" was immensely helpful, and your suggestions, like "less of a travelogue" and "more Buffy – maybe dialogue" and "keep the focus" – were important to my efforts. You gave me a sense of purpose when I was discouraged and a sense of pride in what I was trying to do. As a memoirist "consultant" you are the best!

Elizabeth (Buffy) Cooke,
Author, *Life Savors*

Marcia Rosen
marciagrosen@gmail.com
www.mymemoirworkbook.com
www.creativebookconcepts.com
www.mrosenconsulting.com
516-650-3058 (cell phone)
505-293-2122
Subscribe to my FREE Writers &Self-Publishing E-letter

My Memoir Workbook
By
Marcia Rosen

Edited
By
Terry Z. Lucas

Available:
AbbottPress.com (bookstore)
Amazon. Com
Barnes & Noble.com
MyMemoirWorkbook.com

Printed in the United States
By Bookmasters